Understanding the Elements of the Periodic Table™

NEON

Edward Willett

rosen publishing's
rosen
central®

New York

Published in 2007 by The Rosen Publishing Group, Inc.
29 East 21st Street, New York, NY 10010

First Edition

Library of Congress Cataloging-in-Publication Data

Willett, Edward, 1959–
Neon / Edward Willett.
p. cm.—(Understanding the elements of the periodic table)
Includes bibliographical references and index.
ISBN-13: 978-1-4042-1008-0
ISBN-10: 1-4042-1008-3 (library binding)
1. Neon—Juvenile literature. I. Title. II. Series.
QD181.N5.W55 2006
546'.752—dc22

2006016690

Manufactured in the United States of America

On the cover: Neon's square on the periodic table of elements. Inset: The atomic structure of neon.

Contents

Introduction

In 1923, California businessman Earle C. Anthony returned home to Los Angeles from a trip to Paris, France. With him he had two very expensive signs for his Packard automobile dealership, which was located at Wilshire and La Brea in Hollywood. Once the signs were installed, they snarled traffic for blocks as people drove into town just to look at them. The signs simply read "Packard." But it wasn't what they said, it was how they said it: the signs glowed, in blue and reddish-orange. Someone said they looked like liquid fire.

The signs were basically gas-filled tubes with electrodes at each end. As electric current passed through the gases inside the tubes, the gases glowed. The blue tubes were filled with argon (Ar). The reddish-orange tubes were filled with neon (Ne). They were the first neon signs in North America.

French chemist and inventor Georges Claude displayed the first neon light on December 11, 1910, at the Grand Palais in Paris. Claude's associate, Jacques Fonseque, sold the first commercial sign in 1912 to a Paris barber. In 1913, a sign with letters three and a half feet tall (1.06 meter) reading "CINZANO" (the name of an Italian liquor company) was installed on the avenue Champs-Elysées, and in 1919, the Paris Opera House's entrance was decorated in reddish-orange and blue tubes.

America really took to neon signs. A year after Anthony installed his signs in Hollywood, Claude Neon Lights, Inc., franchises had

The red-orange glow of neon illuminates Radio City Music Hall in New York City. New York took to neon signs early on; by 1927, the city already had 750.

sprung up in several U.S. cities. By 1927, New York City already had 750 glowing gas signs. By the 1930s, more than 5,000 glass benders were employed in more than 2,000 neon workshops across the country, creating the intricate glass tubes for what became known as neon signs, even though only the ones that glowed reddish-orange contained neon. It was all pretty impressive for an element that is both inert and almost undetectable.

Chapter One
Neon Is All Around Us

By the late nineteenth century, scientists had a pretty good grasp of the makeup of air. They knew it contains oxygen (O), of course, and they knew that the rest of air is mostly nitrogen (N).

Back in the eighteenth century, British chemist Henry Cavendish had discovered that air seemed to contain something else. When he conducted an experiment in which sparks were passed through a mixture of nitrogen and oxygen, he found that eventually all the nitrogen and oxygen combined and was used up, but about 1/120 of the volume of the original nitrogen remained.

In the early 1890s, British chemist Lord Rayleigh (born John William Strutt) found that nitrogen extracted from the air was a little denser than nitrogen extracted from ammonia (an alkaline compound of nitrogen and hydrogen, NH_3). This also implied that there must be something in the air no one had identified yet.

After hearing Rayleigh read a paper on his findings, British chemist William Ramsay asked if he could help solve the mystery. Ramsay passed nitrogen taken from the air over hot magnesium (Mg). The magnesium absorbed all the nitrogen but left behind a gas that had about 1 percent of the original volume.

British physicist William Crookes examined the residual gas using a spectroscope (a device that breaks light into its constituent colors)

Sir William Ramsay is pictured here in his laboratory around 1904. Ramsay, working with Morris William Travers, isolated neon, krypton, and xenon from liquid air.

and determined it was not nitrogen. Rayleigh and Ramsay continued to experiment with the new gas leading up to a presentation to the Royal Society, the most important scientific organization in Great Britain, in January 1895. They couldn't get it to chemically combine with anything. It seemed to be inert. Reflecting that, they called the new gas argon, which comes from a Greek word meaning "inactive." They knew from its relative density that it made up about 0.934 percent of air. But that still left 0.034 percent of the gases in air unaccounted for.

Spectroscopy

When elements are heated, they give off light. Just as white light is made up of all wavelengths (colors) of light mixed together, the light given off by a particular element is also a mixture of wavelengths. The wavelengths present in a light source are called its spectrum. The spectrum of white light is what we see in a rainbow. Each element, when heated, produces light with its own unique spectrum.

To see that spectrum, scientists use a spectroscope. At the heart of the spectroscope is either a prism of glass or a diffraction grating, which passes light through fine, closely spaced slits. Prisms and diffraction gratings both break light into its constituent wavelengths, producing a series of colored lines. By examining these lines, scientists can determine which elements are present in a particular subject. Spectroscopy (studying matter and energy by examining the spectra they produce) is a useful tool for determining the chemical makeup of all kinds of scientific subjects, from rocks to gases to distant stars.

The Discovery of Four Elements

In 1898, Ramsay, working with chemist Morris William Travers, set out to find what might be in that remnant of atmosphere. They fractionally distilled liquid argon, that is, allowed it to evaporate slowly. Because different elements have different boiling points, they knew any elements mixed in with the argon should boil off separately.

Three years earlier, in 1895, Ramsay had isolated helium (He) from gases emitted from a uranium-bearing mineral called cleveite. (Before that, helium was only known from spectroscopic analysis of the sun's atmosphere.) Like argon, helium was an inert gas. Based on their similarities and atomic weights, Ramsay thought they must be the first two elements in a new and previously unsuspected group in the periodic table. He also knew there should be another element between them in that group, one lighter than argon but heavier than helium. He also knew that finding it would be difficult. "Here is a supposed gas," he wrote, "endowed no doubt with inert properties, and the whole world to find it in."

But to their surprise, the first gas Ramsay and Travers identified on May 30, 1898, was heavier than argon rather than lighter. They called it krypton (Kr), from the Greek *kryptos*, meaning "hidden."

In June, they modified their experiment. This time they started with solid argon, surrounded by liquid air. Again they allowed it to evaporate under reduced pressure. The first gas that came off, they put into their atomic spectrometer. Heated, it glowed a brilliant crimson color they'd never seen before. Spectroscopy and other tests proved they had, indeed, found the element between helium and argon that they'd been looking for.

Ramsay's thirteen-year-old son Willie said, "What are you going to call the new gas? I should like to call it *novum*." (*Novum* is the Latin word for "new.") Ramsay liked the idea, but because the names of the other

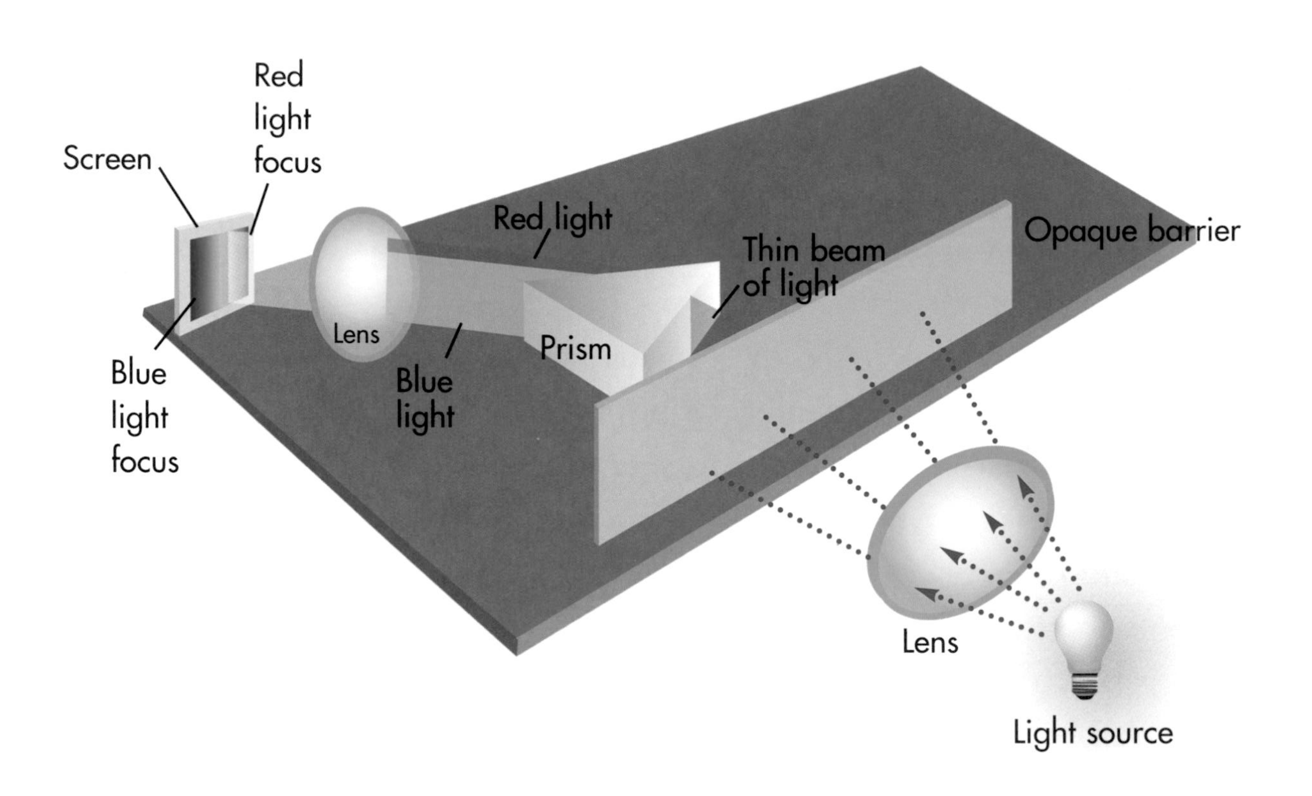

A simple spectroscope is illustrated above. A slit in the opaque barrier allows a thin beam of light to pass through a prism, which splits it into its component colors. A lens focuses the light into a sharp image.

inert gases were based on Greek, he decided to start with *neos*, the Greek word meaning "new." He called the new gas neon.

The very next month, working with liquefied krypton, Ramsay and Travers found another new element. This element was even heavier than krypton; they called it xenon, from the Greek word for "stranger," *xenos*.

The Birth of Neon Lights

Just a few years before Ramsay and Travers isolated neon, krypton, and xenon, an American inventor named Daniel McFarlan Moore developed

The Discovery of Neon in the Words of Morris William Travers

"The blaze of crimson light from the tube told its own story, and it was a sight to dwell upon and never to forget. It was worth the struggle of the previous two years; and all the difficulties yet to be overcome before the research was finished. The undiscovered gas had come to light in a manner that was no less than dramatic. For the moment, the actual spectrum of the gas did not matter in the least, for nothing in the world gave a glow such as we had seen."

—From *A Life of Sir William Ramsay* (1956)

an electric lamp that consisted of a glass tube filled with carbon dioxide and nitrogen. Electrodes at both ends of the tube passed a current through the gases, causing them to glow bright white.

Shortly after the turn of the century, Parisian inventor Georges Claude was looking for a use for the inert "waste gases" that were produced when oxygen was extracted from the air. (The oxygen was used primarily by hospitals and welding shops.) Claude experimented by filling some Moore lamps with neon and argon—and discovered that they produced bright reddish-orange and blue glows, respectively.

Today, we understand why. Normally, electrons surround the nuclei of atoms at certain specific energy levels, sometimes called electron shells or electron orbits. The high voltage applied to the gas in a neon lamp (as high as 14,000 volts, boosted from ordinary household current by small transformers) partially ionizes it—that is, it frees electrons from some of the gas atoms, enabling them to carry electric current. As these free electrons rush from one electrode to the other down the length of the tube,

Dr. E.F.W. Alexanderson (1878–1975), one of the early pioneers in the development of television, examines a special neon lamp used in an early electromechanical television set.

they collide with other gas atoms, moving their electrons briefly to a higher energy level. When these excited electrons fall back to their normal level, they release energy in the form of photons (particles of light). The wavelength, or color, of that light is specific to whatever kind of gas is involved. Thus, neon produces a reddish-orange glow, argon (with the addition of a little mercury vapor) a brilliant blue glow, helium a straw or yellow-white glow, and krypton a silver-white glow.

Although these gases were "inert," meaning that they didn't combine with other elements, they could still be put to good use. But it was their quality of inertness that earned them their own group in the periodic table of the elements.

Chapter Two
Neon and the Other Nobles

The ancient Greek philosopher Democritus suggested, sometime around 400 BC, that all matter is made of minute particles. He called these particles atoms and said they are the smallest possible pieces into which matter can be divided. (The word "atom" comes from a Greek word that means "that which cannot be divided.")

About 2,200 years later, scientists realized that each of the elements—the basic substances that cannot be separated into simpler substances, no matter how much you bend, bang, heat, melt, or pulverize them—had its unique atoms. Their experiments also showed that the most important property of an atom is its mass, or weight. If the lightest element known, hydrogen (H), was given an atomic weight of one, then all other elements had atomic weights that were close to being multiples of one.

In the mid-1800s, some scientists listed all the known elements by weight and discovered that every eighth one was similar. So, they attempted to arrange the known elements into a table that reflected this discovery. One of these scientists was Russian chemist Dmitry Mendeleyev (also spelled Mendeleev), who published his version in 1869. There were gaps in his table that he said would be filled as new elements were discovered. Because of the "periodic" similarities that cropped up every eight atomic weights, he even made predictions about the missing elements' characteristics. The three gaps he specified were all filled in the next few years, and the elements that

Dmitri Mendeleyev *(left)* created the periodic table of the elements. His version is emblazoned on the side of a technical school *(above)* in St. Petersburg, Russia.

filled those gaps had characteristics close to those he had predicted. Mendeleyev's version of the table thus became the most widely accepted one, and he is usually credited as the father of the "periodic table of elements." However, it has been revised and extended considerably since his time.

Scientists had learned that atoms are made up of subatomic particles called protons, neutrons, and electrons. Protons, with a positive charge, and neutrons, with no charge, form a heavy nucleus at the center of the atom. Electrons, with a negative charge, surround the nucleus in energy-specific shells, or layers. The atomic weight of an element is determined by the total number of its protons and neutrons. (The electrons are so much

The most common form of neon, diagrammed here, has ten protons and ten neutrons in its nucleus, and ten electrons in two electron shells. Because its outermost electron shell is full, neon is chemically inert.

smaller that their weight doesn't really matter much.) Atomic weight is also called atomic mass, and it is measured in atomic mass units (amu). The most common form of neon has an atomic weight of 20.1797 amu. This number has been rounded to two digits, 20, in our periodic table because it has 10 protons and 10 neutrons in its nucleus. (Atomic weight is an average weight—atoms of an element are not always identical.) The atomic number of an element is simply the number of protons in its nucleus. Neon's atomic number is 10.

Isotopes Discovered

Elements can exist in a variety of isotopes. Each isotope of an element has the same number of protons in its nucleus, but a different number of neutrons.

Neon played an important role in the discovery of isotopes. In 1909, Francis William Aston moved to the Cavendish Laboratory at Cambridge University in Cambridge, England, to work with Professor J. J. Thomson, who had discovered the electron in 1897. Thomson had developed a method of measuring atomic weights that involved using a combination of electrical and magnetic fields to cause positively charged particles to produce curves on a photographic plate. When Aston and Thomson experimented with neon, they saw two curves instead of one. This

Neon Snapshot

10 20
Ne

Chemical Symbol:	Ne
Classification:	Noble gas
Properties:	Colorless, odorless, tasteless gas; glows reddish-orange in a vacuum tube; Cavendish, Priestley, and others called it "burnt or dephlogisticated air," which meant air without oxygen
Discovered By:	William Ramsay and Morris William Travers, in 1898
Atomic Number:	10
Atomic Weight:	20.1797 atomic mass units (amu)
Protons:	10
Electrons:	10
Neutrons:	10
Density at 68°F (20°C):	0.838 grams per liter (g/l)
Melting Point:	–415.46°F (–248.59°C)
Boiling Point:	–410.94°F (–246.08°C)
Commonly Found:	In air (18 millionths [18 parts per million, ppm] of the volume of Earth's atmosphere)

implied that the neon they were working with was actually made up of two different kinds of atoms that had the same chemical properties, but different weights. It was the first demonstration of the existence of multiple stable isotopes of an element.

The most common isotope of neon is called neon-20 (the mass number after the hyphen is the total number of protons and neutrons in the isotope's atom). The second isotope Aston and Thomson identified was neon-22. Today, we know there is also a third isotope that occurs naturally, called neon-21. (Aston and Thomson did not discover it because there is far less of it than the other two.)

Several short-lived radioactive isotopes of neon have also been created. Many radioactive isotopes have been made by bombarding naturally occurring isotopes of an element with neutrons or protons to introduce an extra neutron or proton into the nucleus. This can create an unstable version of the element that emits radiation as it transmutes, or changes, itself into a stable version. The radioactive isotopes of neon currently have no commercial or scientific uses.

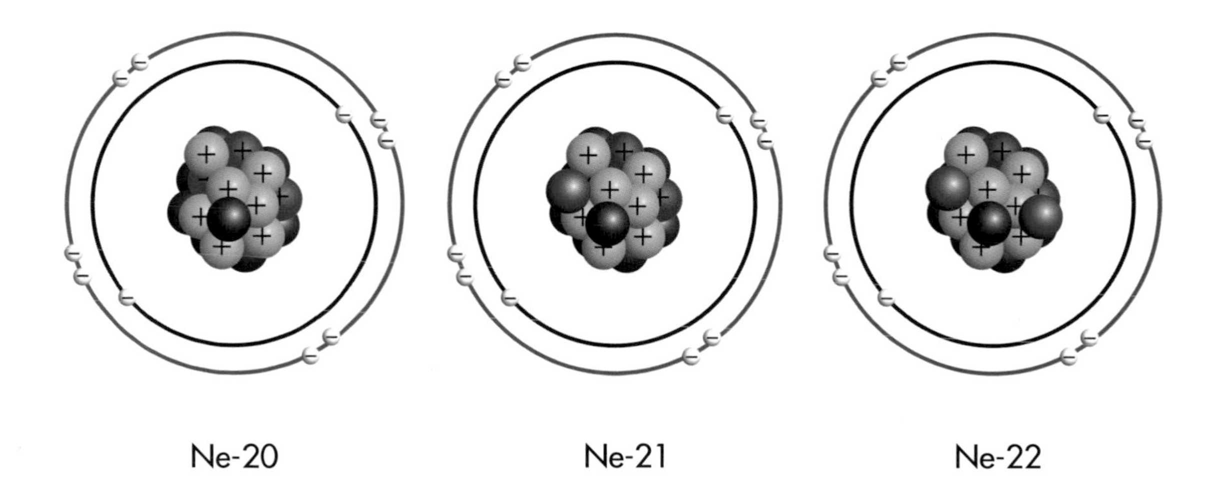

Neon occurs naturally in three isotopes. Neon-20, the most common, has ten protons and ten neutrons. Neon-21 has eleven neutrons, and Neon-22 has twelve neutrons.

Periods and Groups

Each of the energy levels, or electron shells, that electrons inhabit within an atom can only contain a certain number of electrons. The properties that make each element unique depend primarily on how many electrons in its outer shell, called valence electrons, are available to interact with the valence electrons of other atoms.

Within each electron shell, electrons inhabit sub-shells, which scientists have labeled *s, p, d,* and *f.* The *s* sub-shell can hold only two electrons, the *p* sub-shell can hold six, the *d* sub-shell can hold ten, and the *f* sub-shell can hold fourteen. Higher energy levels can hold more sub-shells. Energy level one has just one sub-shell, energy level two can have two sub-shells, energy level three can have three sub-shells, and energy levels four and above can have all four.

The rows of the periodic table are called periods. As you move across the period from left to right, each element has one more proton and one

Why Are They Called Noble?

Before people knew about noble gases, they had heard of noble metals. These are metals, like gold (Au), silver (Ag), and platinum (Pt), that don't react easily with other elements. Therefore, they don't readily corrode or rust, unlike the base metals iron (Fe) and copper (Cu), for example. They also tend to be very valuable, so they became associated with aristocrats, or the nobility.

Because there was already a group of noble metals in the periodic table, it made sense that the new inert gases should also be called noble. They may also be called noble because, like the nobility, they hold themselves aloof and don't mingle.

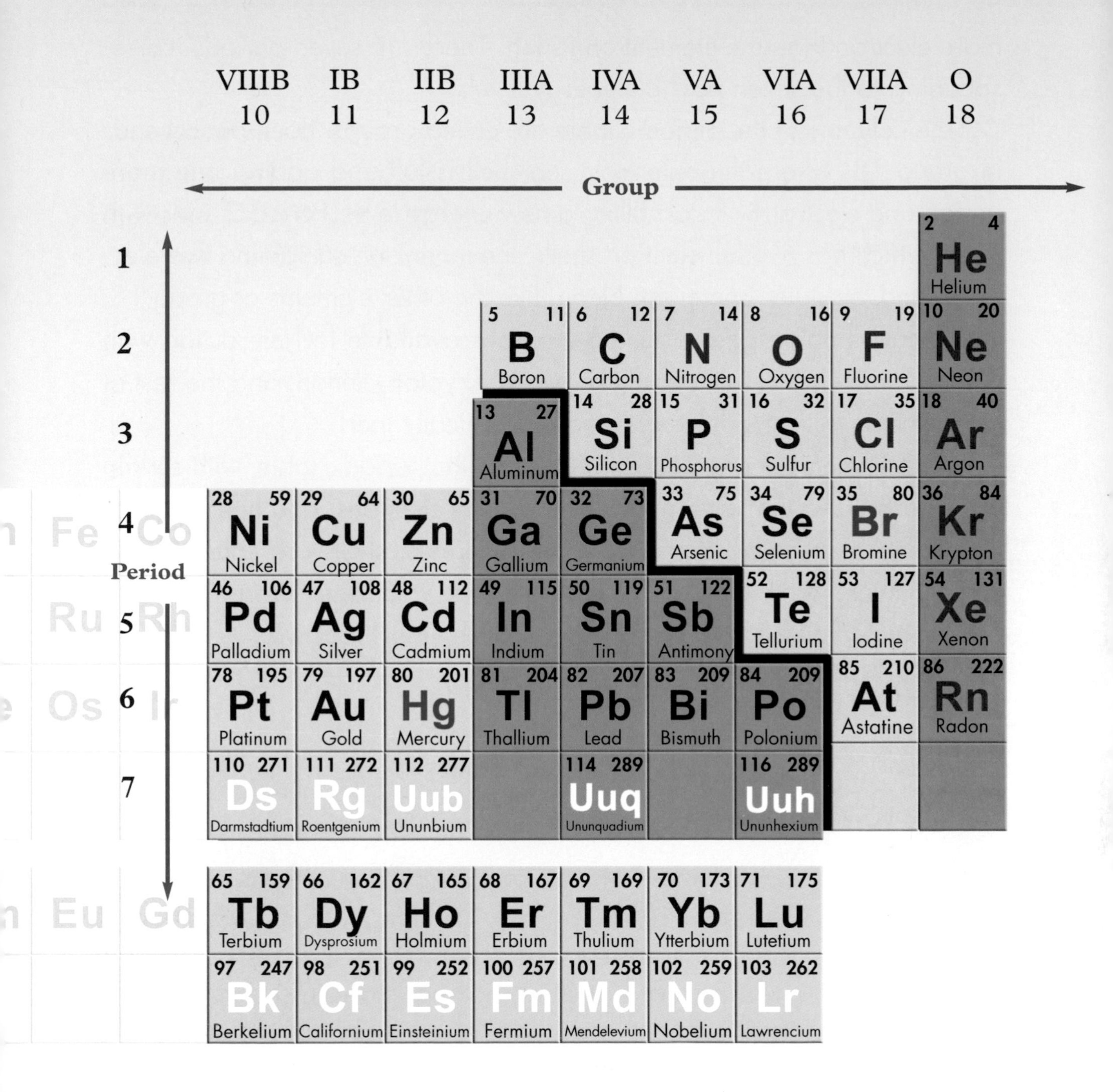

Part of the periodic table of the elements is shown here. The noble gases, including neon, form the rightmost column, or group.

more electron than the element on its left. There are seven periods, corresponding to the seven possible energy levels.

The columns of the periodic table are called groups. Each period ends in group 18, where the outermost sub-shell is full and adding one more proton and electron will start filling a new energy level. Period 2 ends with neon, which has two full electron shells, the inner one containing two electrons, and the outer one eight. Neon, like the other elements of group 18, the so-called noble gases, has no electrons available for interaction with other atoms. As a result, neon (like argon, krypton, xenon, and the rest of the elements in its group) is essentially chemically inert.

Most elements of any particular group in the periodic table, with certain exceptions, have the same number of valence electrons, and hence similar properties. In general, elements whose outermost shells are either almost empty (lithium, for example, which has just one valence electron) or almost, but not quite, full (such as chlorine [Cl]) are the most reactive.

The Noble That Wasn't

In 1999, a team of scientists at Lawrence Berkeley National Laboratory (Berkeley Lab) at the University of California campus in Berkeley announced that they had observed Element 118, temporarily dubbed ununoctium and given the symbol Uuo, in the decay products from targets of lead bombarded with an intense beam of high-energy krypton ions. Ununoctium would have fallen into group 18 below radon on the periodic table. However, in 2001, the team retracted its original paper because follow-up experiments at Berkeley and elsewhere failed to reproduce their results. So, Element 118 so far remains unobserved.

Because the number of electrons in an element's atom is determined by the number of protons in the nucleus, taking away or adding just one proton from the nucleus of an element would turn it into a completely different element with completely different properties. Neon has an atomic number of 10. If you took away just one proton, you would have fluorine (F), a gas that, far from being inert, is highly reactive and dangerous. Neon is part of the atmosphere, and we breathe it harmlessly all the time. Fluorine gas is so poisonous that breathing it at a concentration of only 0.1 percent for just a few minutes is fatal. (Fluorine is so reactive that under certain conditions, it will even form compounds with some noble gases—but not with neon.)

If, on the other hand, you add just one proton to neon's nucleus, you don't get a gas at all. Instead, you get sodium (Na), a soft, silvery-white metal that is so reactive it sometimes bursts into flame when placed on water.

The first noble gas discovered, argon, posed difficulties for the periodic table. The evidence collected by Ramsay and Rayleigh indicated that if the new gas was indeed a new element, it had to have an atomic weight of nearly 40. That placed it between potassium (K) and calcium (Ca) on the periodic table of that time—and there was no gap for it there.

But with the discovery of additional inert gases—first helium, then krypton, neon, and xenon—it became obvious that a whole new group was needed in the periodic table. (Argon is not placed between potassium and calcium in the modern periodic table because today's table is based on atomic number, not atomic weight. Argon, whose atomic number is 18, instead appears between chlorine, atomic number 17, and potassium, atomic number 19.) Consequently, Ramsay has the honor of being the only scientist involved in the discovery of almost an entire group of the periodic table. (He didn't discover radon [Rn], the heaviest of the gases in the group, but he did help determine its atomic weight.) Ramsay won the 1904 Nobel Prize in chemistry "in recognition," according to the Royal Swedish Academy of Sciences, "of his services in the discovery of the inert gaseous elements in air, and his determination of their place in the periodic system."

Chapter Three
There's Something in the Air

Someday, we may run short of certain substances (oil, for instance) as the ready supply of them is used up. Neon isn't one of them. There are other substances whose collection, use, and disposal poses huge environmental problems (for example, oil). Neon isn't one of these, either. Neon, as noted earlier, was first discovered in the air. It makes up around eighteen parts per million of the atmosphere. That means there isn't very much of it in even a large volume of air. On the other hand, there's a very great deal of air on the planet, so worldwide there are more than 72 billion tons (68 billion metric tons) of neon.

It's even rarer in the earth's crust, where it makes up about seventy parts per trillion. It's the eighty-second most common element in the crust, which is another way of saying it's extremely rare.

Neon is actually rarer on Earth than it is in the rest of the universe. In the universe as a whole, it's the fifth most abundant element in the atmosphere. That's because neon is produced in stars much more massive than the sun as part of the process of nuclear fusion (the process in which the nuclei of two lighter elements are united to form a heavier nucleus with the release of large amounts of energy).

Since neon is all around us in the air, when we want pure neon, that's where we get it—although we have to liquefy the air to do this. In fact, we get neon from the air using essentially the same method that

Carl von Linde, a German engineer, invented a method of liquefying air and separating out its components.

Ramsay and Travers used to discover the element.

Liquefying Air

German engineer Carl von Linde found a way to liquefy air in 1895, by first compressing it, then letting it expand rapidly. When gases expand rapidly, they cool—in this case, enough to turn the air into liquid. In 1902, Linde figured out how to separate air's main compounds, oxygen and nitrogen, by slowly warming liquid air. Oxygen and nitrogen boil off at different temperatures and can be extracted as they do so. But so do argon, neon, krypton, and xenon. For Linde, these were little more than waste products. He was mainly interested in oxygen, which was needed in acetylene torches for cutting and welding metal. Today, however, these waste gases are often extracted for various industrial uses.

Neon's boiling point is so low, at –410.94° F (–246.08° C), that it doesn't condense into a liquid with the air. Instead, it remains as a gas, mixed with helium, the boiling point of which is even lower, and some nitrogen. By increasing the pressure and reducing the temperature, the nitrogen can be removed: it condenses back into a liquid and can be adsorbed by highly cooled charcoal. The neon is then separated from helium by using highly cooled activated charcoal: both gases are adsorbed by the charcoal, then released at different temperatures as the charcoal is warmed. It takes 88,000 pounds (40,000 kilograms) of air to produce one pound (0.45 kg) of neon. Nevertheless, neon is relatively inexpensive, costing about $7.60 per gallon ($2 per liter).

There's no danger that we will ever run short of neon. Only a few tons of it, on average, are used commercially in a year. In addition, since it's

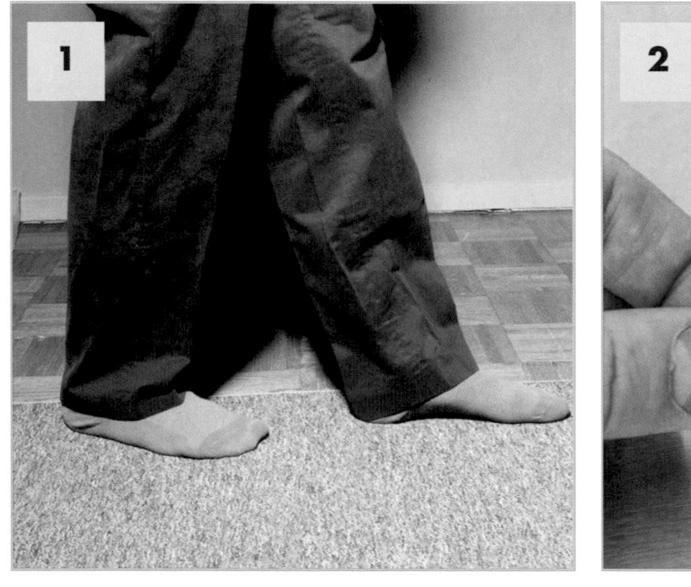

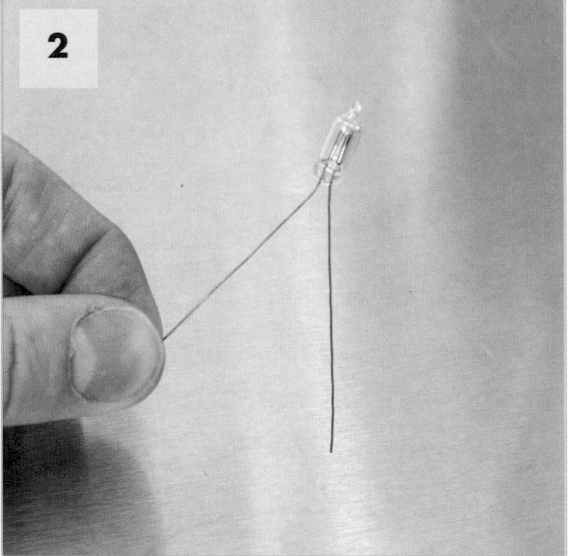

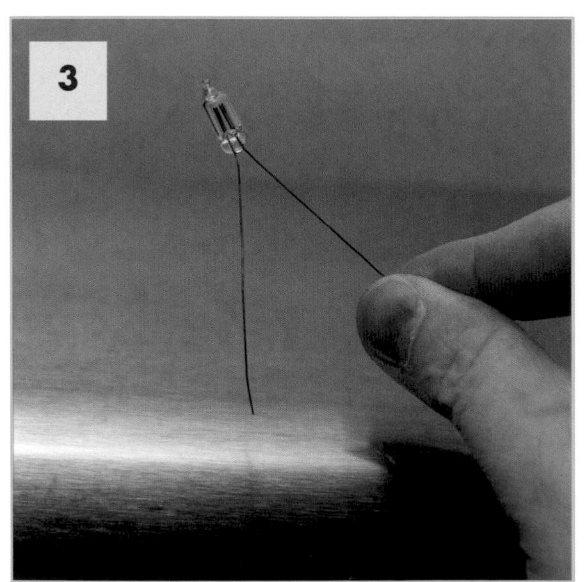

The bulb above contains a tiny amount of neon gas. If you shuffle your feet on the carpet *(photo 1)* while holding one of the bulb's wires *(photo 2)*, then touch the other wire to a ground point like a water pipe or metal file cabinet *(photo 3)*, you should see a brief flash in the bulb. The static electrical charge you accumulated by shuffling your feet passes through the neon gas, exciting it and causing it to glow.

chemically inert, almost all the neon used commercially will eventually find its way back into the atmosphere unchanged, ready to be extracted again.

The fact that it's chemically inert also means that neon is not a danger to the environment, although it can be dangerous to those who work with it. Liquid neon is so cold that contact with it can cause severe frostbite. Neon is not poisonous, but it can't support life, either. Liquid neon, when it turns back to a gas at room temperature (68°F [20°C]), expands 1,445 times—the most of any known liquefied gas. If this happens in an enclosed space, the expanding neon can quickly drive out most of the air.

"They Say the Neon Lights Are Bright on Broadway"

"They say the neon lights are bright on Broadway" is the first line of a song by Jerry Leiber and Mike Stoller that was made popular by the Drifters in 1963. The main industrial use of neon gas is in neon lights.

Long before there were neon lights, people knew that you could make gas glow. As early as 1675, French astronomer Jean Picard noticed that when he shook a mercury barometer tube, it glowed faintly. Picard didn't know why, but today we know that static electricity was causing mercury vapor in the tube to light up.

By 1855, a German glassblower named Heinrich Geissler was making "Geissler tubes." When electricity was applied to low-pressure gas (at first simply air, though other gases such as neon were used later) in the tubes, the tubes would glow. Different gases produced different colors.

In the 1890s, U.S. inventor Daniel McFarlan Moore developed a lamp that consisted of a glass tube filled with carbon dioxide and nitrogen. Electrodes at both ends of the tube passed a current through the gases, causing them to glow bright white. The gas inside was consumed quickly, giving the tubes a short lifespan, so Moore invented an automatic refilling

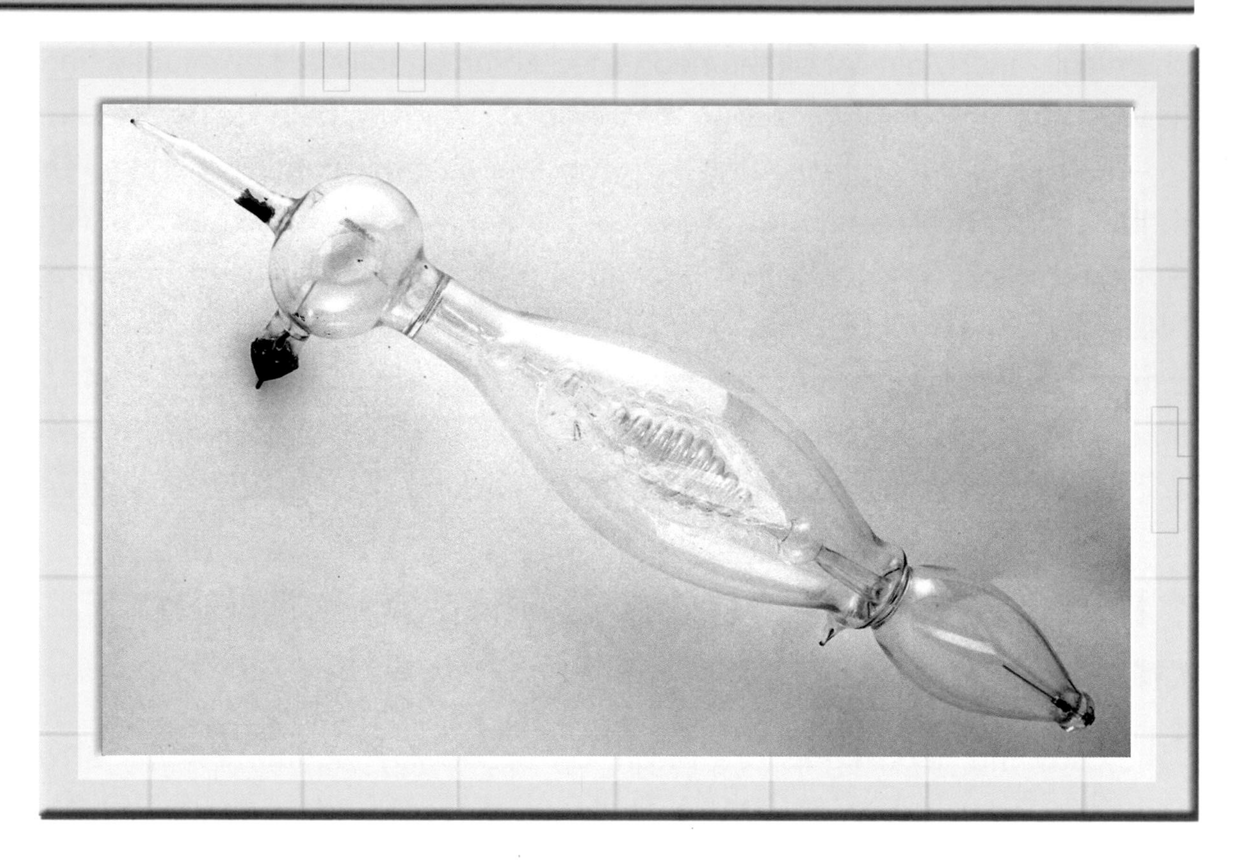

Geissler tubes like this one were first made in the 1850s. Electricity passing through a low-pressure gas in the central tubing causes it to glow. Different gases produce different colors. Geissler tubes were made both for use in scientific research and for purely decorative purposes.

valve that could refill a tube during operation if its pressure dropped. The first luminous advertising sign using Moore lamps went up on a hardware store in Newark, New Jersey, in 1904.

After Carl von Linde figured out how to liquefy air and thus made it easy to produce inert gases, French inventor Georges Claude began experimenting with them in the hope of improving the Moore lamp. He reasoned that the gas in a Moore lamp didn't last because it was reacting with the electrodes at each end of the tube. If that were true, then an inert gas should last longer because it wouldn't react with anything.

Claude found that neon glowed brighter with less electrical input than any of the other gases he tried. He first displayed his neon light in 1910.

More on Moore

Daniel McFarlan Moore began his career in lighting working for Thomas Edison, who famously perfected the incandescent light bulb. Moore felt that new techniques for sealing glass might make a light based on glowing gas—already demonstrated by the Geissler tube—commercially viable.

Not surprisingly, Edison wasn't wild about the idea; he didn't want anything else competing with his light bulb. He's reported to have asked Moore, "What's wrong with my lamp?" to which Moore replied, "It's too small, too hot, and too red." Not long after that, Moore was working for himself and created the Moore lamp in 1898. In 1920, he invented the glow lamp, a low-powered neon- or argon-filled lamp, which was used in instrument panels and appliances until the invention of LEDs (light-emitting diodes) in the 1970s and is still used in some night-lights today.

Just two years later, the first commercial neon sign was sold by his company, Claude Neon. Claude's neon lighting tube was patented in the United States on January 19, 1915, and made its debut in Los Angeles, California, in 1923.

Neon lights are made essentially the same way today as they were by Georges Claude. First, the glass tubing is shaped. After that, it must be processed using a procedure called bombarding, which removes gases absorbed onto the glass's inner surface. In bombarding, much of the air is pumped out of the tube, then a high-voltage current is passed through it until it reaches a temperature of 550°F (288°C).

After that, more air is pumped out of the tube until it is almost completely empty. Then it is filled with neon.

A neon sign maker is working with glass tubes. A skillful sign maker can create all kinds of striking text and imagery from carefully shaped glass tubes.

Colors of light other than neon's red-orange are most often produced by a mixture of argon gas and mercury vapor, combined with a phosphorescent coating on the inside of the glass tube (a coating that glows when bombarded with electromagnetic radiation). Argon glows a vivid blue, while the mercury vapor gives off ultraviolet light that makes the coating glow brightly in one of a variety of available colors.

Different colors can also be produced by using different gases. Krypton glows a dim blue, while xenon has a blue-white glow. Colored tubing can also produce unique colors.

Many of the colors currently seen in neon lights were the result of research in the 1950s on color television. Engineers at RCA's laboratory in Princeton, New Jersey, needed materials that would glow in very intense colors when struck by the beam of electrons that creates the television picture on the inside of a picture tube. The phosphors still used in color televisions' (and, later, computer monitors') cathode ray tubes (CRTs) helped spark a renewed interest in neon lights in the 1960s.

Since the 1960s, neon has become an art form. More than 400 artists have displayed their work at the Museum of Neon Art in Los Angeles, and "neon" has become an English adjective meaning something brightly colored.

Just remember—the only neon lights that actually contain neon are those that glow reddish-orange.

Chapter Four
More Than Just a Pretty Light

Neon lights are the most famous use of neon, but they're certainly not the only use for the element. Another important use is in helium-neon lasers.

On May 15, 1960, a cylindrical rod of synthetic ruby placed inside a spiral flash lamp momentarily produced light 10 million times more powerful than sunlight. The experiment, conducted by American physicist Theodore H. Maiman in his laboratory at Hughes Aircraft Company in California, had produced the first laser. ("Laser" is an acronym for Light Amplification by Stimulated Emission of Radiation.)

Today, lasers have a host of applications, from eye surgery to CD players to light shows at rock concerts. There are many different types. The original ruby laser was an example of a solid-state laser, one that generates laser light from a solid. Excimer lasers produce ultraviolet light from a mixture of reactive gases such as chlorine and fluorine and inert gases such as argon, krypton, or xenon. Dye lasers, which use complex organic dyes, can be tuned to produce laser light at many different wavelengths (one at a time). Semiconductor lasers are all around us: they're used in CD and DVD players and burners, and in laser pointers. Then there are gas lasers, of which the most common are helium-neon (HeNe) lasers.

Remember that the light in a neon lamp comes from photons, or particles of light, emitted when electrons drop from a higher energy state, or electron shell, to a lower one. The electrons were briefly placed in the higher energy state by a collision with one of the electrons carrying electrical current through the gas.

A photon can also briefly boost an electron to a higher level. When a photon comes into contact with an atom that has two energy levels with an energy difference exactly equal to the energy of the photon, then the photon may be absorbed, and an electron at the lower level moves up to the higher. The atom is now said to be in an excited state, but it only lasts for a tiny fraction of a second. Then it throws off a photon and returns to a lower energy state.

In 1917, physicist Albert Einstein suggested that if a photon from one atom came into contact with a similar atom that was already in an excited state, it could cause the excited atom to release another identical photon. This is called stimulated emission.

Lasers basically consist of three items: a material that acts as a light amplifier (the ruby rod in Maiman's original laser, for example, or the gas in a helium-neon laser), a source of energy (such as Maiman's flash lamp—it's usually light or electricity), and two mirrors. The energy source excites the atoms in the light amplifier (called the active medium) so that they can produce emission. The energy source has to be strong enough to excite the atoms faster than they can decay back to their normal state in order to create what is known as a population inversion, where there are more excited atoms than non-excited ones.

Initially a few atoms emit photons spontaneously, and those photons stimulate other atoms to emit identical photons, too. Through stimulated emission, the number of photons quickly increases. Some of the photons go out the sides of the active medium and are lost, but some travel the length of the medium, inducing still more atoms to emit. When they reach the end of the active medium, they bounce off one of the mirrors and return to stimulate still more atoms. In this way a single photon can produce millions and millions of others exactly like itself in practically no time at all.

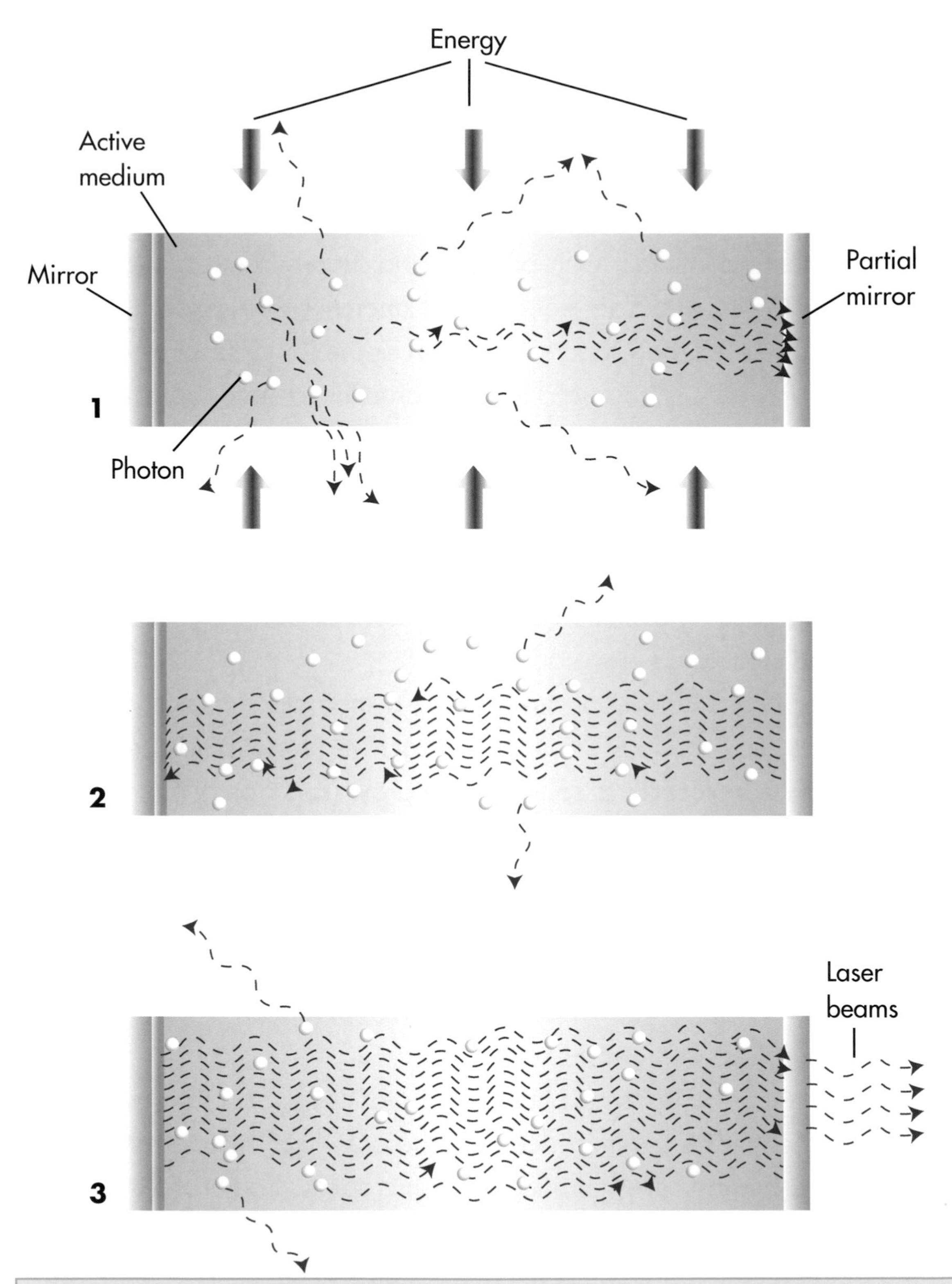

This is how a laser works. In figure 1, energy excites the active medium, causing it to produce photons. In figure 2, while some photons escape out the sides, others bounce back and forth between the mirror and the partial mirror, stimulating the medium to produce even more photons. In figure 3, when enough photons have been produced, some escape through the partial mirror as a laser beam.

Although one mirror is a regular, fully reflecting mirror, the other is only partially reflecting. It allows some light to pass through. That light is the laser beam.

Laser light is special in several different ways. First, it is monochromatic (all one, pure color). That's because all the photons in the laser, being identical copies of one another, have exactly the same wavelength.

Laser light is also coherent. This means that those identical light waves (sometimes it's easier to describe light as being made up of particles, sometimes of waves) are exactly in step with each other. The crest of each wave is lined up with the crest of every other wave. You can have monochromatic

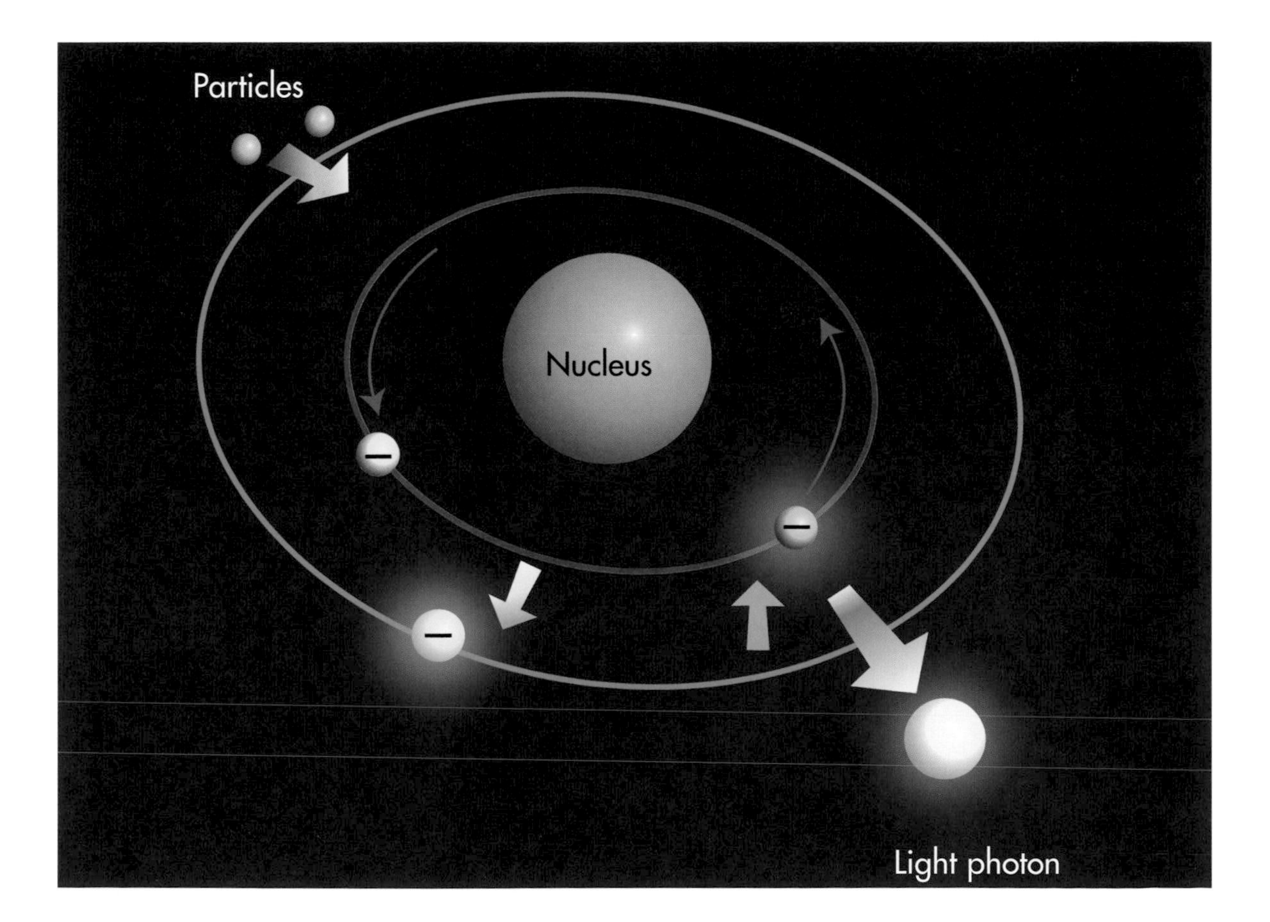

This illustration shows how an atom emits light. Particles striking an atom boost an electron to the next highest shell. When the electron drops back to its usual shell, it releases its excess energy as a photon.

light that is incoherent, where the waves aren't in step with each other. Normal white light is not only incoherent, it's also non-monochromatic, containing light at many different wavelengths.

Ali Javan, a physicist at the Massachusetts Institute of Technology (MIT), constructed the first helium-neon laser in 1960. In a helium-neon

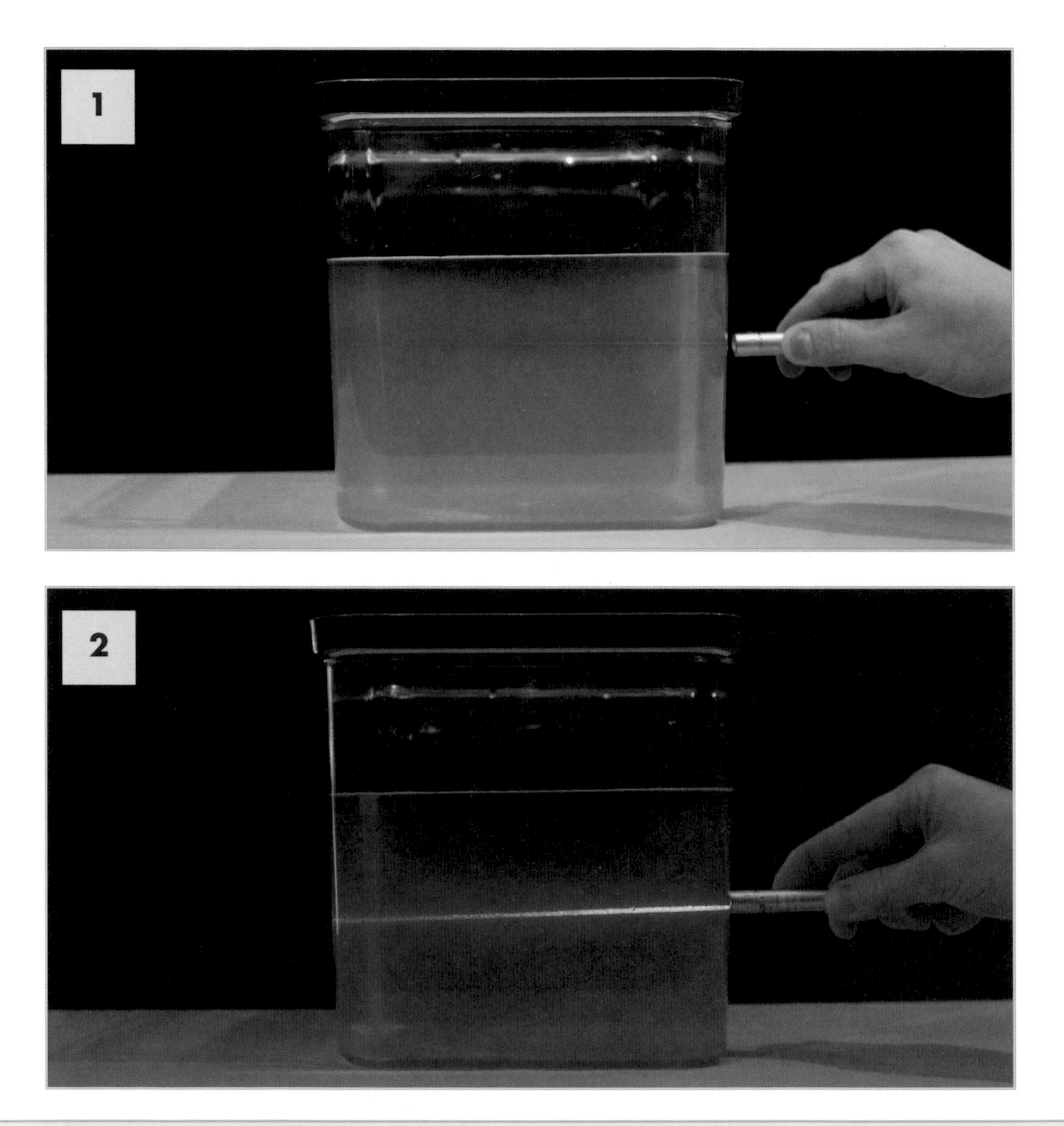

Laser beams, like other forms of light, are invisible until they reflect off an object. In photo 1, a tank of water has been placed in front of a black background. In photo 2, after turning off the lights, a helium-neon laser is shone through a tank of water mixed with a little cornstarch. The laser light reflects off of the cornstarch particles, allowing you to see it.

laser, electrodes transfer electrical energy to the helium-neon gas mixture. The electrical energy ionizes the helium atoms, which then transfer their energy to the neon atoms, causing them to emit light. Although the most common color of light emitted by a helium-neon laser is red, there are also helium-neon lasers that emit green light and even some that emit invisible infrared light.

The most visible usage of helium-neon lasers is in retail stores, where their red light is used to read bar codes on merchandise, providing computerized cash registers with information about what has just been sold and what to charge for it.

Neon and TV

Today, neon is used in high-tech plasma screens, but it was also used in the earliest televisions, which didn't use electronics at all. In fact, they were mostly mechanical!

In a standard television, what you're actually seeing is a single point of light of varying intensity "painting" the inside of the TV tube from side to side and top to bottom so rapidly that our brains, thanks to something called "persistence of vision," perceive it as a full-screen image.

In an old-style electromechanical TV camera, a disk with a series of holes spiraling in toward the center spins rapidly. A photoelectric cell inside the camera reacts to the varying strength of the beam of light coming through the holes in the disk and turns it into a varying electrical current that can be transmitted to a receiving unit.

In the receiver, the current is used to vary the intensity of a light source. A viewer looks through a small viewing window at this flickering light while a disk identical to that in the camera, and synchronized with it, spins past. The result is a spot of varying light that moves from top to bottom as the holes spiral down, and side to side as the disk turns. The viewer's persistence of vision does the rest, creating the illusion

A face is shown on an electromechanical television designed by John Logie Baird in 1926. A neon lamp was an integral part of the first TVs.

of a full image. The light source of choice for electromechanical televisions was a neon tube, because neon lights react so quickly and sensitively to changes in electrical current.

Plasma TVs generate an image in an entirely different way—but they, too, make use of neon's propensity to glow when excited by electricity. Color video images are made up of pixels (picture elements). On an ordinary television, these pixels are generated by a beam of electrons that lights up colored phosphorescent dots on the inside of the screen. In a plasma television, these pixels are created by tiny fluorescent lights.

Any color of light can be created by mixing the three primary colors of light: red, green, and blue. Each plasma pixel consists of three small cells, each of which produces a different primary color. Hundreds of thousands of these cells are filled with neon and xenon gas. When electricity is applied to the gas, it becomes a plasma, which is a gas made up of electrically charged atoms (called ions) and free electrons.

The cells are sandwiched between plates of glass and connected to two long electrodes, one behind, on the back plate, and one (which is transparent) above, on the front plate. The front electrodes, called the display electrodes, are arranged in horizontal rows across the screen, while the back electrodes, called the address electrodes, are arranged in vertical columns. The two sets of electrodes thus form a grid.

To apply a charge to a particular cell of gas, the plasma display's computer sends a current along the electrodes that intersect at that cell. This causes the neon and xenon mixture to glow. Most of the light produced is ultraviolet, which is invisible. But each cell is coated with a phosphor that produces either red, green, or blue visible light when excited by ultraviolet light. By varying the charge flowing to the various cells—something it does thousands of times every fraction of a second—the plasma display's computer mixes the primary colors as required to create an ever-changing light display that we see as full-color, full-motion video.

Other Uses for Neon

People have found a number of other uses for neon over the years. In the 1930s, for instance, airports marked their runways with neon lights because the reddish-orange glow shone through fog and haze better than other colors. (Today, most runways are marked with krypton-filled lights, which emit very bright blue-white flashes.)

At the heart of a Geiger counter, a device used to detect radiation, is a Geiger-Muller tube. This is a tube filled with an inert gas—typically neon or argon—and (in some cases) an organic vapor. A metal or metal-coated outer wall serves as the negatively charged electrode (the cathode). A wire passing up the center of the tube serves as the positively charged electrode (the anode). When radiation passes through the tube, it ionizes some of the gas molecules. Positively charged ions are drawn toward the cathode, and negatively charged electrons are drawn toward the anode. As the ions rush one way and the electrons the other, they ionize additional gas atoms along the way. The result is a short, sharp surge of electrical current that typically is used to generate

Geiger counters like this one are used to detect radiation, which they typically indicate with a loud click. The more clicks, the higher the radiation count. At their heart is a tube filled with an inert gas such as neon.

a click. The more clicks the Geiger counter emits, the higher the level of radiation.

Neon-filled tubes are used as electronic switches. Under normal circumstances, a neon-filled tube acts as an insulator, so no current flows through it. But when there is a surge of voltage, the neon tube fires—the gas inside is ionized, the tube lights up, and electricity is able to pass through it. In a voltage regulator, this characteristic of neon is used to bleed away excess voltage before it can damage anything. In specialized tubes like the thyratron, this is used to instantly switch current to a different electronic circuit as required. This kind of neon-tube switch is much faster than a mechanical switch would be.

Liquid neon is often used as a cryogenic refrigerant. The word "cryogenics" means both the study of and the production of extremely low temperatures. (Generally, temperatures that are below –238°F [–150°C].) Liquid neon has a lower boiling point than any gases except helium and hydrogen, and although it's not quite as cold as they are, its greater density means that it has three times the refrigerating capacity of liquid hydrogen by volume and more than forty times the refrigerating capacity of liquid helium.

Scientists at Yale University in New Haven, Connecticut, are currently studying the use of liquid neon as a detection medium for neutrinos. These mysterious particles carry no electrical charge and have very little mass, which means they pass through ordinary matter as if it weren't there. They're produced by the sun (and other stars), and trillions of them zip harmlessly through your body every second. The earth itself is pretty much transparent to neutrinos.

CLEAN (Cryogenic Low Energy Astrophysics with Noble Gases) is a project, still very much in the early experimental stage, to fill a large vat with liquid neon and watch for the very rare flashes of ultraviolet light produced when a neutrino interacts with an electron or a nucleus of a neon atom. Studying these flashes can tell us more about neutrinos—specifically, how much mass they have and how much energy they carry as they hurtle away from the sun. Learning more about neutrinos may teach us more about how stars such as our own sun work, and may even provide clues as to the ultimate fate of the universe.

It would be appropriate if neon, produced in the furnaces of stars and the fourth most common element in the universe, were to help us solve the deepest mysteries of the universe. That would be a pretty impressive achievement for an inert gas most people think of in terms of a red-orange sign reading "GOOD EATS."

The Periodic Table of Elements

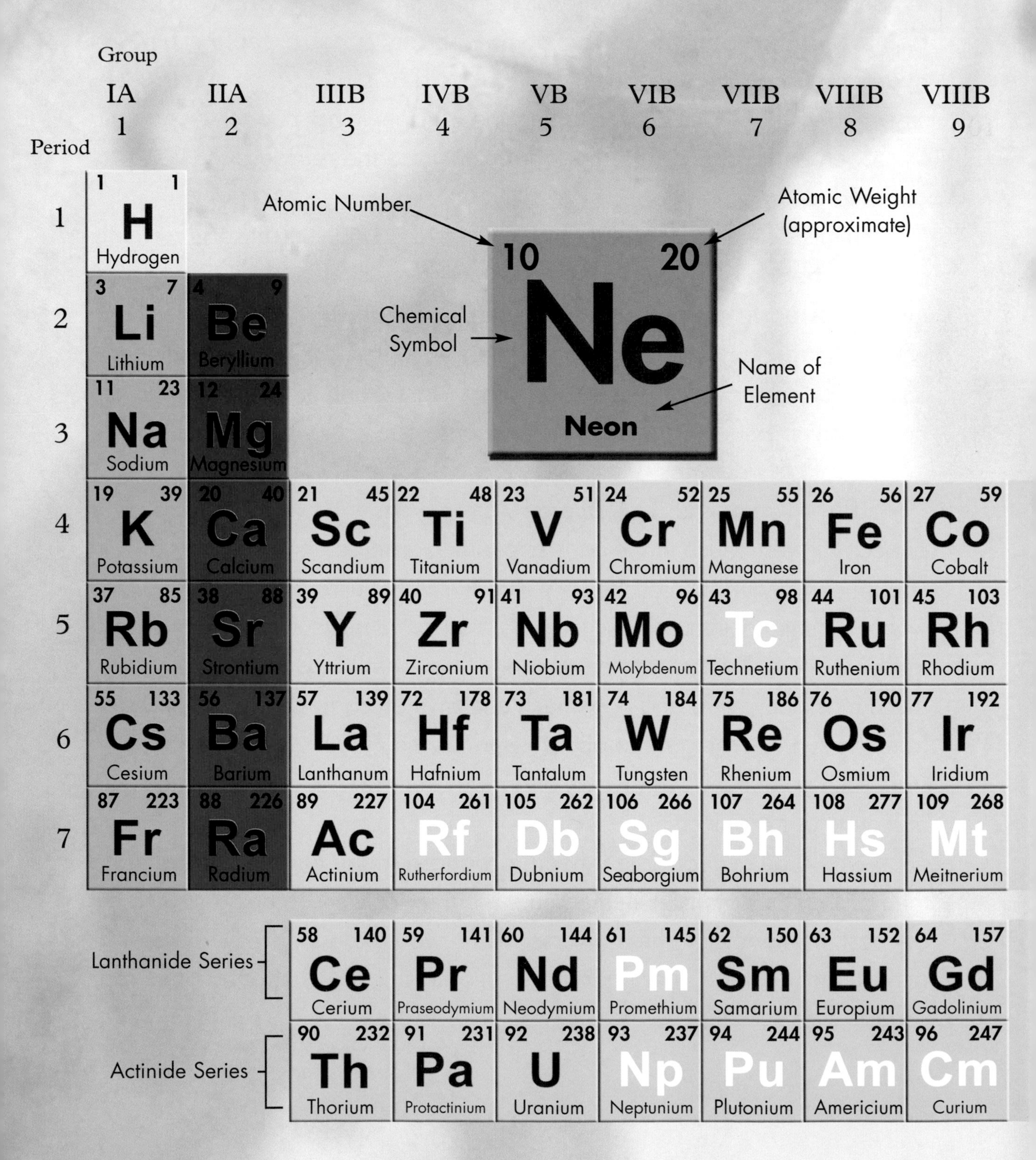

Group

Period	IA 1	IIA 2	IIIB 3	IVB 4	VB 5	VIB 6	VIIB 7	VIIIB 8	VIIIB 9
1	1 H Hydrogen 1								
2	3 Li Lithium 7	4 Be Beryllium 9							
3	11 Na Sodium 23	12 Mg Magnesium 24							
4	19 K Potassium 39	20 Ca Calcium 40	21 Sc Scandium 45	22 Ti Titanium 48	23 V Vanadium 51	24 Cr Chromium 52	25 Mn Manganese 55	26 Fe Iron 56	27 Co Cobalt 59
5	37 Rb Rubidium 85	38 Sr Strontium 88	39 Y Yttrium 89	40 Zr Zirconium 91	41 Nb Niobium 93	42 Mo Molybdenum 96	43 Tc Technetium 98	44 Ru Ruthenium 101	45 Rh Rhodium 103
6	55 Cs Cesium 133	56 Ba Barium 137	57 La Lanthanum 139	72 Hf Hafnium 178	73 Ta Tantalum 181	74 W Tungsten 184	75 Re Rhenium 186	76 Os Osmium 190	77 Ir Iridium 192
7	87 Fr Francium 223	88 Ra Radium 226	89 Ac Actinium 227	104 Rf Rutherfordium 261	105 Db Dubnium 262	106 Sg Seaborgium 266	107 Bh Bohrium 264	108 Hs Hassium 277	109 Mt Meitnerium 268
Lanthanide Series			58 Ce Cerium 140	59 Pr Praseodymium 141	60 Nd Neodymium 144	61 Pm Promethium 145	62 Sm Samarium 150	63 Eu Europium 152	64 Gd Gadolinium 157
Actinide Series			90 Th Thorium 232	91 Pa Protactinium 231	92 U Uranium 238	93 Np Neptunium 237	94 Pu Plutonium 244	95 Am Americium 243	96 Cm Curium 247

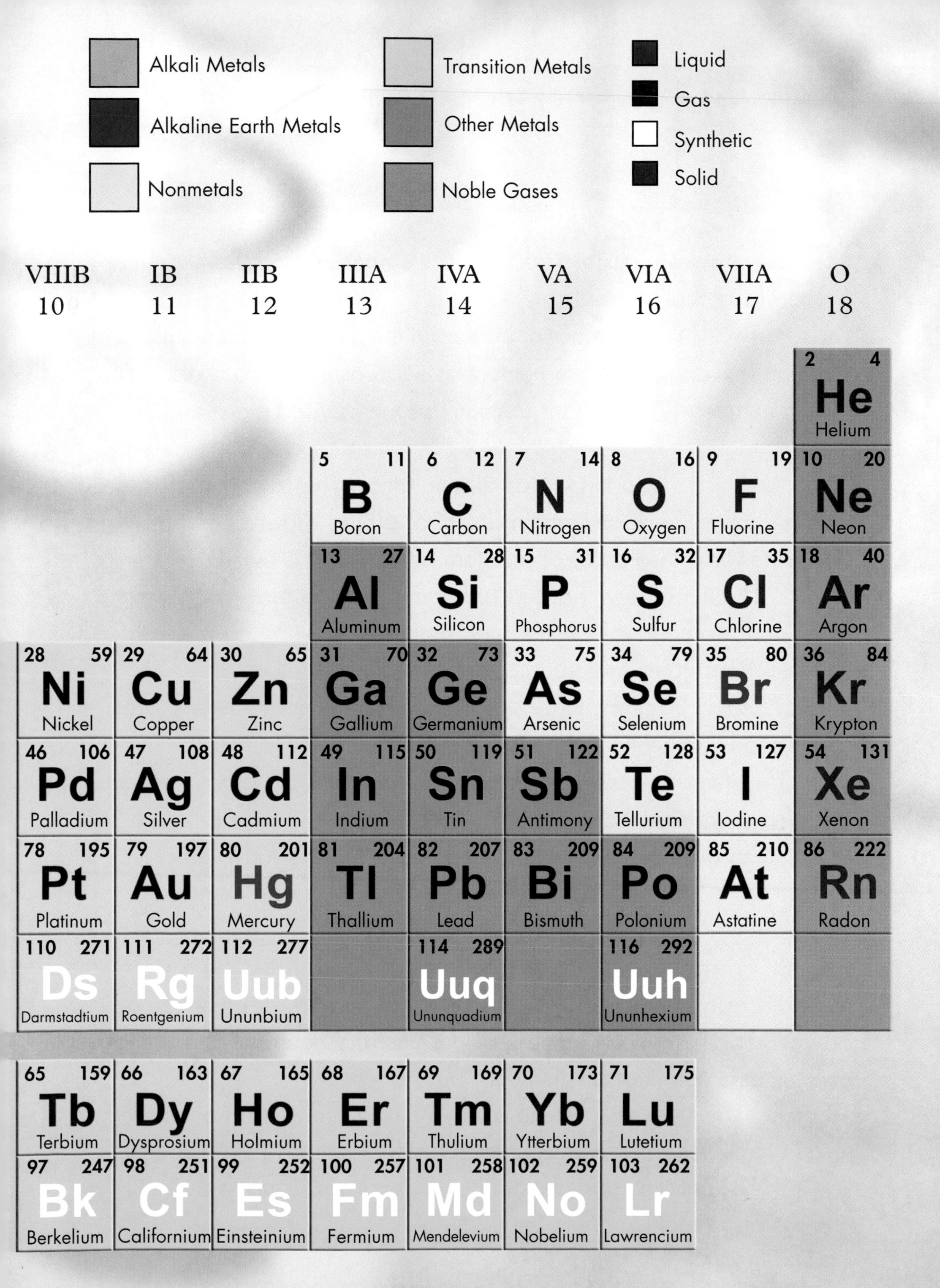
Alkali Metals
Alkaline Earth Metals
Nonmetals
Transition Metals
Other Metals
Noble Gases
Liquid
Gas
Synthetic
Solid
VIIIB 10
IB 11
IIB 12
IIIA 13
IVA 14
VA 15
VIA 16
VIIA 17
O 18
2 4 He Helium
5 11 B Boron
6 12 C Carbon
7 14 N Nitrogen
8 16 O Oxygen
9 19 F Fluorine
10 20 Ne Neon
13 27 Al Aluminum
14 28 Si Silicon
15 31 P Phosphorus
16 32 S Sulfur
17 35 Cl Chlorine
18 40 Ar Argon
28 59 Ni Nickel
29 64 Cu Copper
30 65 Zn Zinc
31 70 Ga Gallium
32 73 Ge Germanium
33 75 As Arsenic
34 79 Se Selenium
35 80 Br Bromine
36 84 Kr Krypton
46 106 Pd Palladium
47 108 Ag Silver
48 112 Cd Cadmium
49 115 In Indium
50 119 Sn Tin
51 122 Sb Antimony
52 128 Te Tellurium
53 127 I Iodine
54 131 Xe Xenon
78 195 Pt Platinum
79 197 Au Gold
80 201 Hg Mercury
81 204 Tl Thallium
82 207 Pb Lead
83 209 Bi Bismuth
84 209 Po Polonium
85 210 At Astatine
86 222 Rn Radon
110 271 Ds Darmstadtium
111 272 Rg Roentgenium
112 277 Uub Ununbium
114 289 Uuq Ununquadium
116 292 Uuh Ununhexium
65 159 Tb Terbium
66 163 Dy Dysprosium
67 165 Ho Holmium
68 167 Er Erbium
69 169 Tm Thulium
70 173 Yb Ytterbium
71 175 Lu Lutetium
97 247 Bk Berkelium
98 251 Cf Californium
99 252 Es Einsteinium
100 257 Fm Fermium
101 258 Md Mendelevium
102 259 No Nobelium
103 262 Lr Lawrencium

Glossary

atom The smallest possible part of an element having the chemical properties of that element.

atomic number The number of protons in the nucleus of an atom of an element. This also equals the number of electrons in a neutral atom. The atomic number determines an element's properties and place on the periodic table.

atomic weight Also known as atomic mass. The average of the weights (or more accurately, masses) of all the different naturally occurring forms (isotopes) of an atom of a specific element.

electron The negatively charged subatomic particle that, with others of its kind, occupies the space in an atom surrounding the nucleus.

element A substance made up of only one kind of atom.

free electrons Electrons that have broken free from atoms and are moving independently. Free electrons carry electrical current.

group The elements in a vertical column of the periodic table. Elements in a group typically have similar properties.

ion An atom or a molecule that has a positive or negative electrical charge from having temporarily acquired or lost one or more electrons.

isotopes Forms of an element the atoms of which have the usual number of protons, but more than the usual number of neutrons.

mass number The total number of protons and neutrons in the nucleus of an atom of an element.

molecule The smallest particle of an element, consisting of one or more atoms, that exists on its own and still maintains its properties.

neutron A subatomic particle that has no charge, found in the nucleus of an atom.

nucleus The positively charged central portion of an atom, made up of protons and neutrons, where most of the atom's mass is concentrated.

period In the periodic table, each horizontal row of elements.

phosphor A substance that glows when struck by electrons or ultraviolet light.

plasma A form of gas that freely conducts electricity because many of the electrons orbiting its nuclei have become energized enough to break free of the atoms.

proton A positively charged subatomic particle found in the nucleus of an atom.

valence electrons The electrons in the outer shell of an atom. The interaction of valence electrons allows atoms to link together chemically and metals to conduct heat and electricity.

For More Information

The Museum of Neon Art
501 West Olympic Boulevard, Suite 101
Los Angeles, CA 90015
(213) 489-9918
Web site: http://www.neonmona.org

Thomas Jefferson National Accelerator Laboratory
Office of Science Education
628 Hofstadter Road, Suite 6
Newport News, VA 23606
(757) 269-7560
Web site: http://education.jlab.org

Web Sites

Due to the changing nature of Internet links, Rosen Publishing has developed an online list of Web sites related to the subject of this book. This site is updated regularly. Please use this link to access the list:

http://www.rosenlinks.com/uept/neon

For Further Reading

Ball, Philip. *The Ingredients: A Guided Tour of the Elements.* New York, NY: Oxford University Press, 2002.

Emsley, John. *Nature's Building Blocks: An A-Z Guide to the Elements.* New York, NY: Oxford University Press, 2001.

Newton, David E. *Chemical Elements: From Carbon to Krypton.* Detroit, MI: U•X•L, 1999.

Saunders, Nigel. *Neon and the Noble Gases (The Periodic Table).* Chicago, IL: Heinemann, 2003.

Bibliography

The BBC. "History of Chemistry—Noble Gases." March 17, 2003. Retrieved April 2006 (http://www.bbc.co.uk/dna/h2g2/A1000792).

Bellis, Mary. "The History of Neon Signs." Retrieved April 2006 (http://inventors.about.com/library/weekly/aa980107.htm).

Caba, Randall. "Finding the Neon Light." SignIndustry.com. Retrieved April 2006 (http://www.signindustry.com/neon/articles/2003-10-30-RC-FindingtheNeon.php3).

Chemical Achievers. "William Ramsay." Retrieved April 2006 (http://www.chemheritage.org/classroom/chemach/periodic/ramsay.html).

Harris, Tom. "How Plasma Displays Work." HowStuffWorks.com. Retrieved April 2006 (http://electronics.howstuffworks.com/plasma-display.htm).

Hudson, John. "A Noble Discovery." *Chemistry and Industry*, August 15, 1994. Retrieved April 2006 (http://www.highbeam.com/library/doc0.asp?DOCID=1G1:15728657&num=1&ctrlInfo=Round20%3AMode20b%3ASR%3AResult&ao=&FreePremium=BOTH).

IAEI.org. "Origins of Neon Light." Retrieved April 2006 (http://www.iaei.org/subscriber/magazine/00_e/neon.htm).

Lasershandbook.net. "Helium-Neon Lasers." Retrieved April 2006 (http://lasershandbook.net/tubes/index.html).

The McKinsey Group. "Cryogenic Low Energy Astrophysics with Noble Gases." Retrieved April 2006 (http://mckinseygroup.physics.yale.edu/clean/).

Nobelprize.org. "Sir William Ramsay—Biography." Retrieved April 2006 (http://nobelprize.org/chemistry/laureates/1904/ramsay-bio.html).

Thielen, Marcus. "Happy Birthday, Neon!" *Signs of the Times*, December 2001, pp. 20–26. Retrieved April 2006 (http://www.signmuseum.com/exhibits/histories/neonbirthday.html).

University College London Department of Chemistry. "The Chemical History of the UCL Chemistry Department—The Discovery of Neon and Other Gases." Retrieved April 2006 (http://www.chem.ucl.ac.uk/resources/history/chemhistucl/hist15.html).

Van der Krogt, Peter. "Elementymology & Elements Multidict." Retrieved April 2006 (http://www.vanderkrogt.net/elements/).

Voynick, Steve. "Five Bright Nobles." *World and I*, March 1, 2000. Retrieved April 2006 (http://www.highbeam.com/library/doc0.asp?DOCID=1G1:59458191&num=1&ctrlInfo=Round20%3AMode20b%3ASR%3AResult&ao=&FreePremium=BOTH).

Weschler, Matthew. "How Lasers Work." HowStuffWorks.com. Retrieved April 2006 (http://science.howstuffworks.com/laser.htm).

Index

About the Author

Edward Willett remembers being fascinated with the neon signs he saw in small towns throughout the Great Plains when, as a boy, he and his parents made annual car trips from Saskatchewan to Missouri, Kansas, Oklahoma, and Texas. Today, Willett, the author of many nonfiction books for children, lives in Regina, Saskatchewan, where he writes a weekly science column for newspapers and radio.

Photo Credits

Cover, pp. 1, 10, 15, 17, 19, 32, 33, 40–41 by Tahara Anderson; p. 5 © Rudy Sulgan/Corbis; p. 7 © Corbis; p. 12 © Underwood & Underwood/Corbis; p. 14 © Steve Raymer/Corbis; p. 14 (inset) © Hulton Archive/Getty Images; p. 23 courtesy Linde AG; pp. 24, 34 by Mark Golebiowski; p. 26 © Index Stock Imagery, Inc.; p. 28 © John Maher/Index Stock Imagery, Inc.; p. 36 © SPL/Photo Researchers, Inc.; p. 38 © Hank Morgan/Photo Researchers, Inc.

Special thanks to Jenny Ingber, high school chemistry teacher, Region 9 Schools, New York, New York, for her assistance in executing the science experiments illustrated in this book.

Designer: Tahara Anderson; Editor: Kathy Kuhtz Campbell